WHITE-WATER SPORTS

by Deb Pinniger

ticktock

D1144088

The author

Deb Pinniger has been kayaking for over 20 years and has spent the last 12 years guiding and competing all over the world full-time. She is twice World Freestyle Champion, European and British Champion. Deb has also competed in extreme races all over the world.

With thanks to: Diana LeCore, Anna Brett, Dixon-Price Publishing, Simon Westgarth and Jason Smith

Thank you to Lorraine Petersen and the members of **nasen**

ISBN-13: 978 1 84898 141 6 pbk
This revised edition published in 2010 by *ticktock* Media Ltd

Printed in China
9 8 7 6 5 4 3 2 1

Picture credits (t=top; b=bottom; c=centre; l=left; r=right):
AFP/Getty Images: 36. Manual Arnu: 22t, 29t, 57b. Bryan & Cherry Alexander Photography/Alamy: 9t. Darren Baker: 32/33t, 54/55t, 54b, 55b. BristolK/Alamy: 35t. Nico Chassing: 15bl. Mike Hamel: 17b, 42, 46. Tommy Hilleke: 61. Tanya Faux: 56b. Erik Jackson: 59cl, 59tr. Kristine Jackson: 56t. Japan Rafters Federation: 30, 31t, 31b. Johnnie Kern: 25c. Jens Klatt: 32b. Cameron Lawson: 33b. John MacGregor, *A Thousand Miles in the Rob Roy Canoe*: 9b. Charlie Munsey/Corbis: 25t. Desre Pickers: 26/27t, 26b, 27bl, 27br. Deb Pinniger: 2, 4/5, 6/7t, 6b, 10/11, 13t, 13cl, 14 all, 15t, 15cr, 16b, 17t, 18/19, 20, 21t, 21b, 28t, 29c, 35b, 37t, 37b, 40/41, 43 all, 44, 45 all, 47t, 48/49, 50/51t, 58t. Aaryn Powell: 52. Robert Preston/Alamy: 24. Geraint Rowlands: 47b. Shutterstock: 1, 3, 7b, 8, 12t, 14/15 background, 53t. Jason Smith: 23c, 38, 39t, 39b. *ticktock* Media Archive: 60. Tom Uhlman/Alamy: 51c. Paul Williams/Action Plus: 16t. Jeff Wolfram/Alamy: 34.

Every effort has been made to trace copyright holders, and we apologize in advance for any omissions.
We would be pleased to insert the appropriate acknowledgments in any subsequent edition of this publication.

CONTENTS

CHAPTER 1: WHITE WATER

Steve Fisher, one of the greatest-ever paddlers, heads towards a massive hole on the Zambezi river, Zambia.

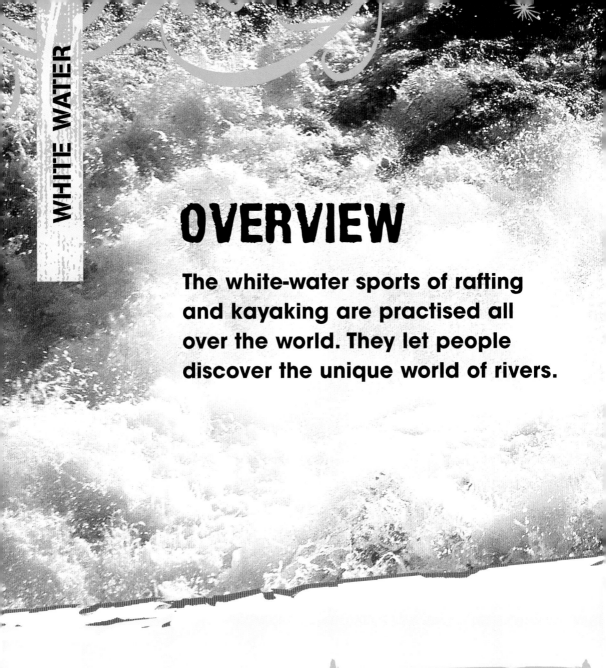

OVERVIEW

The white-water sports of rafting and kayaking are practised all over the world. They let people discover the unique world of rivers.

Paddlers explore all sorts of white water. Some surf big waves, doing tricks in the air. Others run some of the world's largest waterfalls.

Any white-water sport is dangerous, so proper guidance is always needed.

When water moves quickly over rocks, air gets trapped in the water. When the water looks white the stage is set for a lot of fun!

HISTORY

Thousands of years ago, people paddled for survival, using canoes for hunting, fishing and travel.

Early canoes

Ancient canoes were made from natural materials, such as reed. They are still used in some places today on the Nile river in Egypt and on Lake Titicaca, between Bolivia and Peru.

A traditional reed raft on Lake Titicaca

Inuits use their kayaks to fish

Survival

The Inuit of the Arctic invented a closed-cockpit kayak. Covering the top, or cockpit, of the kayak with animal skin stopped the water getting in.

John MacGregor canoeing through Tuttlingen, Germany

Sport

In the 19th century, Briton John MacGregor made canoeing a popular sport in Europe and the USA. He designed a kayak similar to the one used by the Inuit.

CHAPTER 2: THE WATER

Many paddlers set out on long journeys to find the perfect white water. This group are exploring a canyon on the Upper Mendoza river, Argentina.

DIFFICULTY

There are six grades of white water. Grade 1 is the easiest while grade 6 is so difficult that only the best paddlers can survive it.

The grades measure how difficult the water is and how dangerous it can be. It lets the paddler know what skill level they need to run a section of water.

Kayaker Erik Martinsonn crashes into the white foam of the Ulvua river, Norway

More water makes rapids powerful and difficult. When a river is flooded, the fast-flowing water has a lot of power and is dangerous.

Flooded rivers should only be paddled by experts.

The grades vary a lot. The grade of a river can change as the water level rises or falls.

GRADES

Grade 1

This is easy white water. It has a steady current, small waves and simple obstacles.

Grade 2

This reasonably difficult white water has clear passages but the current can change. There are medium-sized waves, holes and obstacles.

Grade 3

The passage is clear but has high waves, holes and boils. There are boulders and other obstacles.

Grade 4

The water pressure is strong with big waves, strong holes, boils, whirlpools, boulders, ledges and drops.

Grade 5

This white water is very difficult. There are high waves with strong holes.

Grade 6

Grade 6 is usually only possible to get through at certain water levels. It is extremely dangerous.

RIVER TYPES

Pool drop

Pool-drop rivers have both rapids and calm water. They are great for people learning to paddle.

Alpine

These rivers are a lot of fun for experienced paddlers.

They are very steep with fast-flowing water from the mountains.

High-volume

These wide rivers have big, bouncy rapids and good surfing waves.

The Nile and Zambezi rivers in Africa are popular with freestyle kayakers.

Steep creeks

These slim rivers are extremely steep. They have lots of drops, waterfalls and slides.

There are a lot of fun, steep creeks in the Italian Alps and in California, USA.

CHAPTER 3:

WHITE-WATER SPORTS

British freestyler Matt Cooke enjoys some paddling on the impressive Falls of Lora, Scotland.

ADVENTURE!

White-water river running is all about sharing adventures and getting to the end together.

Planning and teamwork are needed to run a white-water river. Paddlers go out in groups of three or more people. They tackle the river one section at a time.

Hand signals are often used to communicate because the water is so loud.

Paddlers use strong plastic kayaks for good control and to keep them safe.

Today, paddlers have more control than ever before.

EXPEDITION KAYAKING

The huge white-water of the Indus river, Pakistan

The ultimate white-water adventure, expedition kayaking means travelling down an unknown river.

White-water expeditions take place in remote parts of the world. These rivers are found in thick jungles, hidden canyons or high mountain ranges.

Often the only way to reach these rivers is by kayak.

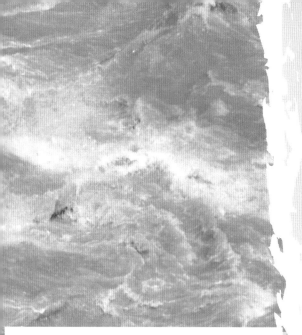

Expedition kayakers take a range of equipment with them, such as:

- video and photographic equipment
- sleeping bags and mats
- tents
- cooking pans and stoves
- food
- satellite phones and maps
- spare paddles
- rescue equipment
- clothes

Camping out on the banks of the Kanali river, Nepal

Paddlers store their supplies and equipment under and behind their kayak's seats. Waterproof bags keep everything dry.

Kayakers have taken part in some incredible white-water expeditions over the years.

The Blue Nile waterfalls near Bahir Dar, Ethiopia

Blue Nile river

In 1972, Britons Mike Jones and Mick Hopkinson led a group down the Blue Nile river in Ethiopia. They ran the biggest rapids ever tried before.

Tsangpo expedition

In 2002, American Scott Lindgren led a 96-person team on the first run of the Tsangpo Gorge in Tibet.

It took place during winter. The river's waters were at their lowest level.

Scott Lindgren watches a section of rapids on the Tsangpo river

The team at Tsangpo river, Tibet, 2002

The Tsangpo Gorge is the deepest river gorge in the world. By running it, Scott and his team made kayaking history.

SOLO KAYAKING

In 2007, South African Hendri Cortez set out to paddle the Murchison Falls section of the White Nile river in Uganda.

It's one of the most dangerous sections of river in the world.

Hendri checks his equipment

Murchison Falls is also famous for its wild animals. There are more hippos in this stretch of river than anywhere else in the world.

Hendri had to prove himself on many grade 5 rapids

Hendri had to move carefully to avoid hippos

RAFTING

White-water rafting is perfect for anyone with a sense of adventure who is looking for an exciting physical challenge. It became a popular sport in the 1970s.

*Preparing for
a big drop*

*The Karakoram
mountains seen from
the Indus river, Pakistan*

Raft trips offer amazing experiences.

Imagine travelling down the Zambezi river in Africa. The only people you'll see are local villagers collecting water and fishermen.

The American river explorer Richard Bangs led expeditions during the 1970s and 1980s that explored some of the world's greatest rivers, including:

- Indus river, Pakistan
- Omo river, Ethiopia

Brazil vs Japan in the 2007 World Rafting Championships sprint

RAFTING COMPETITIONS

Rafting competitions have three events: sprint, slalom and downriver. Each rafting team has six members and a reserve.

Sprint

The sprint is an exciting event to watch. Pairs of teams race down a section of powerful rapids. The sprint counts for 30 per cent of the points.

Slalom

Brazil in the 2003 slalom event

The slalom is the most difficult event. It counts for 30 per cent of the points. Teamwork is needed to get through 12 gates. Touching, failing to pass or moving a gate means a penalty.

Downriver

The downriver event is worth 40 per cent of the points. The racing takes almost an hour along a section of powerful rapids.

Israel and South Africa in the 2001 downriver event on the Zambezi river

CREEKING

The Topolino kayak has made the sport of creek boating possible. It involves paddling down steep waterfalls and low-water creeks.

The Topolino kayak is just 2.2 metres long. Being short means it sits well on the water surface.

Steep waterfalls can only be attempted in a short kayak

Boats with rounded ends like the Topolino are less likely to get stuck on underwater rocks when paddlers jump off waterfalls and drops.

During a big drop, paddlers need to lean forward to absorb the impact of landing and avoid broken bones.

Extreme kayaking races include many big drops

FREESTYLE

Freestyle paddlers perform trick after trick. Each trick requires timing, balance and coordination.

Static water

Freestyle kayakers perform their tricks on a short stretch of static water. The kayakers use small, lightweight kayaks.

Play runs

Most rivers used for freestyle kayaking have small sections known as 'play runs'. Play runs have waves and holes where paddlers can practise.

Championships

Every two years, freestylers from around the world compete at the World Freestyle Championships. The more difficult the moves, the higher the score.

SLALOM

White-water slalom is a race against the clock.

Slalom gates are two poles hung over the river. They are coloured green (downstream) or red (upstream).

Most slalom courses take 80 to 120 seconds to complete. Paddlers compete in teams or solo.

A French team at the 2006 European Slalom Championships, France

Scottish Olympic silver medallist Campbell Walsh at the 2006 European Slalom Championships, France

White-water slalom racing is an Olympic sport. Paddlers race down 300 metres of white water through 20 or 25 gates.

Olympic runs take about 140 seconds to complete.

SQUIRT BOATING

Squirt boating began when slalom racers dipped the backs of their boats under the water. This new move was called a tail squirt.

A squirt boater performing a cartwheel

Squirt boaters use both the river's surface and underwater currents. Paddlers perform many tricks. A cartwheel is where the boat is rotated vertically from end to end.

Squirt boats were developed from slalom boats that had been cut down.

Squirt boats must be light, small and easy to move.

Squirt boats can be custom-built to a paddler's weight and size

CHAPTER 4: THE GEAR

Paddlers need good protection to get through the powerful white water. Paddlers need to stay dry, warm, afloat and visible at all times.

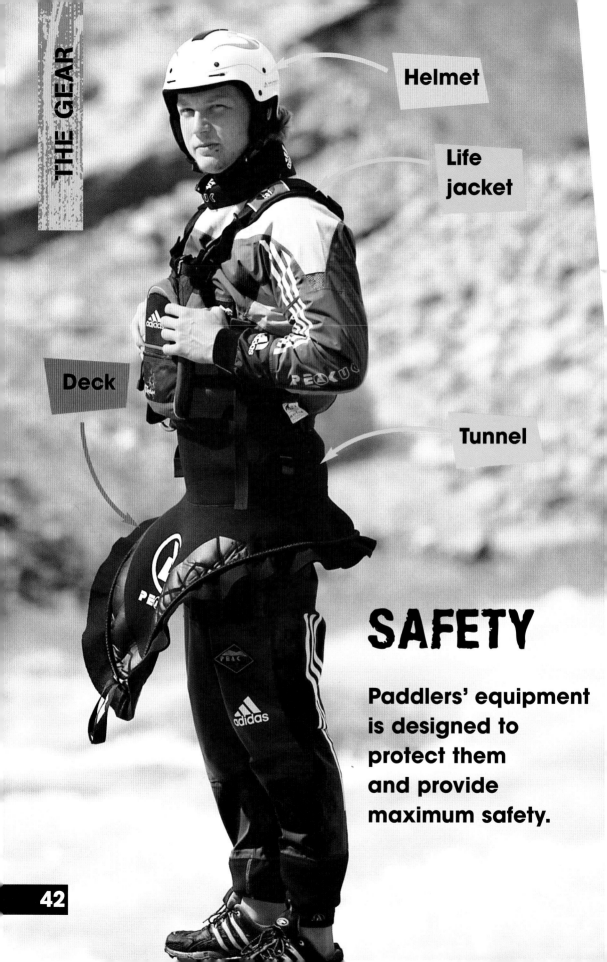

Helmet

Life jacket

Deck

Tunnel

SAFETY

Paddlers' equipment is designed to protect them and provide maximum safety.

Helmet

A helmet is essential for all paddlers. It protects their head from boulders and rocks in the water.

Life jacket

A life jacket's padding protects a paddler from sharp rocks and keeps them afloat if they fall out.

Spray skirt

The spray skirt covers a kayak's cockpit to keep out the water. The paddler wears the tunnel part round their waist.

Safety equipment

A throw rope that floats, a mobile phone and a first aid kit are all essential.

CLOTHING

Shoes

Shoes protect the paddler's feet from cold and sharp rocks. They must provide support and give good grip on slippery rocks.

Dry jacket

Jackets made from a waterproof fabric help keep paddlers dry.

Paddling trousers

Paddling trousers are also made from waterproof fabric. Ankle and waist seals stop the paddler getting wet.

Thermals

Thermal layers and fleeces are worn under jackets and trousers for warmth.

EQUIPMENT

Paddles

Paddles provide power and support in rapids. Many paddles are made from both fibreglass and carbon fibres. These materials make them stiff and light.

Back

Seat

Front

Kayaks

White-water kayaks are made from strong plastic. Foam pillars in the front and back give the boat strength and help to keep its shape.

Rafts

Rafts are made of durable rubber or vinyl fabrics. They are inflated with air to keep them afloat.

In order to avoid punctures, the air is held in separate chambers.

47

CHAPTER 5:

PEOPLE AND PLACES

Tyler Curtis enjoys the spectacular limestone walls of the Grand Canyon of the Verdon, France.

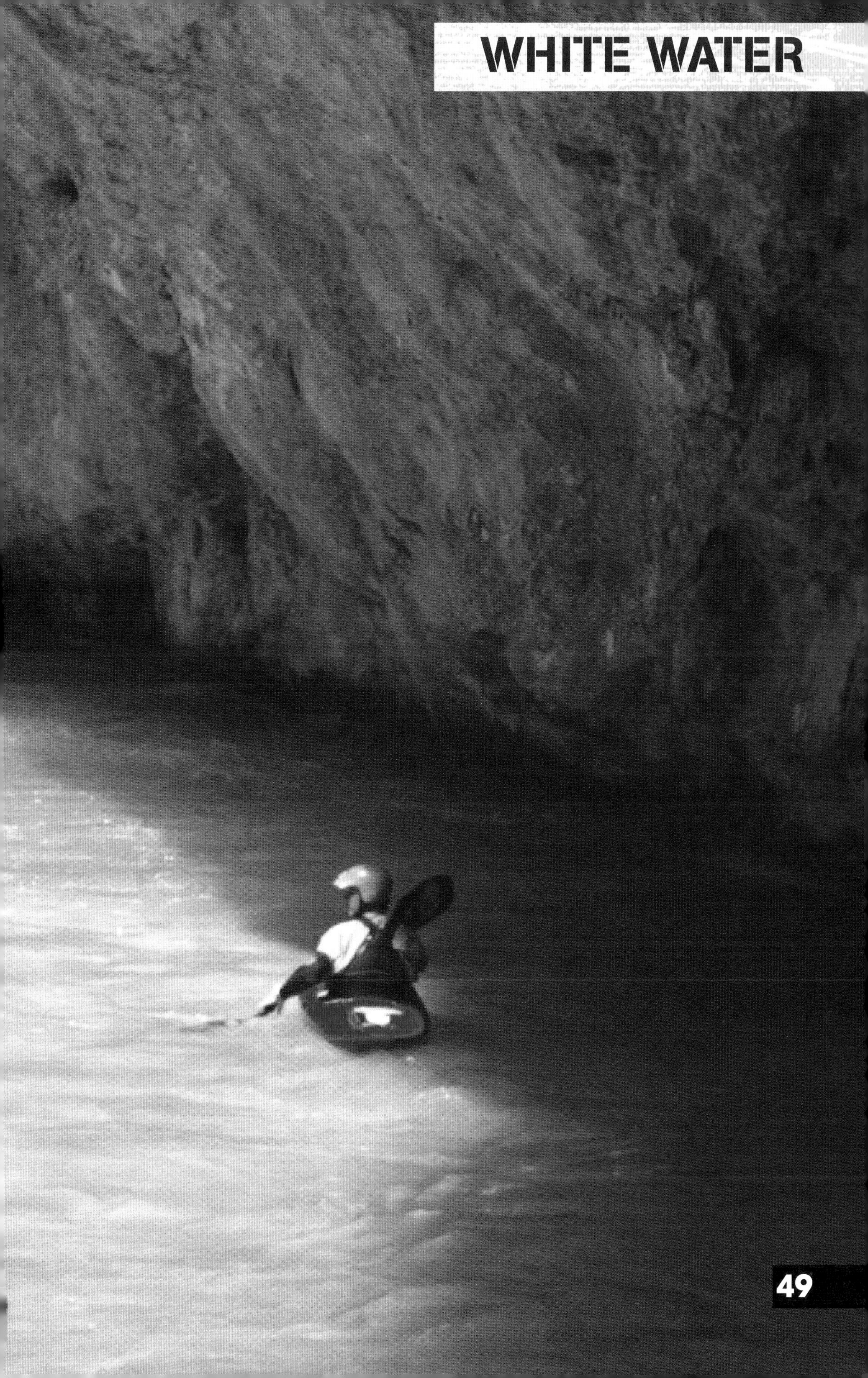

HOT SPOTS

Knowing where to look for the best runs is at the top of every paddler's list.

Africa

Africa offers some of the world's best white-water rivers. The Zambezi river is home to a new paddling style called freeride. Freeride is freestyle mixed with downriver paddling.

Norway

With so many different rivers to choose from, Norway offers something for every paddler – including low-volume, high-volume, waterfalls and big waves.

USA

For six weeks every year, the water level of the Gauley river in West Virginia, USA, is increased to create ideal conditions for paddlers. 'Controlled releases' transform this river into a stretch of grade 4 and 5 white water.

SHAUN BAKER

An extreme kayaker, Shaun Baker is always pushing the boundaries to try something more daring than anyone else!

Shaun has become one of the best freestyle and white-water paddlers. His passion is kayaking big waterfalls.

Shaun on the 12-metre-high Godafoss waterfall in Iceland

Shaun was also
a pioneer of the
land-speed record for
a kayak! He reached a top
speed of 62.9 kilometres per hour.

Shaun's most recent
adventures include
developing a jet-
powered kayak.

*Shaun in his jet-
powered kayak*

AMAZING PADDLERS

Eric Jackson

American Eric Jackson is a master of slalom, extreme racing and freestyle. Eric is an Olympic champion.

Tanya Faux

Nicknamed the T-Bird, Australian freestyle champion Tanya Faux is the best female freestyle paddler in the world.

Niki Kelly

New Zealander Niki Kelly is one of the best female white-water kayakers.

In 2004, she completed the Seven Rivers Expedition in California, USA.

Olaf Obsommer

Germany's Olaf Obsommer is a world-class expedition kayaker.

Olaf has directed some of the most popular films on white-water kayaking.

YOUNG TALENT

Nouria Newman, 15, on her way to fourth place in the women's class at the 2007 French Slalom Championships

White water is full of young talent who push the sport forward.

French kayaker Nouria Newman started paddling when she was five years old. She has been a member of both the French slalom and freestyle teams.

WHITE WATER

Dane Jackson mastering the Bus Eater wave of the Ottowa river, Canada

Emily and Dane Jackson are two of the best junior kayakers in the world. Their father is top kayaker Eric Jackson.

Emily won the title of Junior Women's World Freestyle Champion and Dane came third in the World Freestyle Championships when he was only 14 years old.

Emily Jackson demonstrates a mega-back blunt

JOEY'S STORY

In 1999 US kayaker Joey Kentucky and UK kayakers Andy Round and Simon Westgarth took a trip on the Little White Salmon river in Oregon, USA. This popular river includes the ten-metre-high Spirit Falls.

Joey paddled over Spirit Falls first. The water knocked him over again and again. Exhausted, he fell out of his kayak and floated unconscious down the river.

Andy and Simon chased after Joey. They got hold of him and Simon gave emergency resuscitation. After five minutes Joey regained consciousness.

They climbed out and took Joey to hospital. Doctors found Joey's heart was beating out of rhythm, due to an excess of lactic acid, which caused the heart to stiffen and almost stopped it beating.

Luckily, the slow climb had helped Joey's body transport oxygen to his heart and gradually remove the lactic acid.

It was only due to an experienced team making the right decisions that Joey lives to tell his story!

Simon (left) and Joey (right) a few days after Joey's accident

MILESTONES

1869 – John Wesley Powell explores the Grand Canyon in Colorado, USA, for ten months.

1936 – Canoeing and kayaking on flat water become Olympic sports at the Berlin Games.

1969 – Mike Jones, Jeff Slater, Dave Allen and two others paddle the upper sections of the River Inn, Switzerland, the hardest stretch of water in Europe.

1971 – Walt Blackader tackles the Turnback canyon on the Alsek river, one of North America's most difficult stretches of water.

1972 – White-water slalom takes place at the Munich Olympic Games.

Highest river

The source of Mount Everest's Dudh Kosi river is the Khumbu Glacier, 5.3 kilometres above sea level.

1990 – The first descent of the grade 5 Nevis Bluff rapid on the Kawara river, New Zealand, by Mick Hopkinson.

2002 – Scott Lindgren, Mikey Abbott, Alan Ellard, Johnny and Willie Kern, Dustin Knapp and Steve Fisher paddle the Tsangpo Gorge, Tibet.

2004 – A team of paddlers complete the Seven Rivers Expedition by paddling seven major multi-day trips all on grade 5 water in California, USA, for 50 days in a row.

2007 – German kayaker Felix Lämmler sets a new world record for free-fall kayaking down a waterfall. He descends 34 metres down the Leuenfall waterfall, Switzerland.

All in a day

In 2005, Upper Cherry creek in California, USA, was completed by American paddlers in just one day. Previous attempts had taken three days.

Glossary

Blade The wide piece at the end of a paddle used to push against the water.

Boil A place in the water where two currents meet. The pressure of both currents is very strong, so there is masses of white water.

Boulder A large rock.

Canoe A light, narrow, open boat propelled by one or more paddlers in a kneeling position. Canoeists use single-bladed paddles. They alternate strokes from one side of the canoe to the other.

Canyon A rock gorge with steep sides.

Carbon fibre A synthetic, lightweight material made from woven carbon threads.

Cockpit The space where the paddler sits.

Downstream The direction a river is flowing.

Drop Any spot where flowing water drops suddenly.

Fibreglass A tough synthetic, lightweight material made from glass fibres.

Flat water Calm water found on a slow-moving river or lake.

Gorge A deep, narrow, rocky valley with a river.

Hole A feature in a river where water goes over a rock and returns on itself. Some holes can be life threatening.

Kayak Any of the various boat designs that imitate the Inuit hunting kayak. A kayak has a watertight enclosed top. Kayakers use a paddle with a blade at each end of the shaft.

Lactic acid This is formed in the body's muscles during very heavy exercise, when the need for oxygen exceeds the amount that the body can provide. It stiffens the muscles and causes them to ache.

Ledge The upper lip or edge of a drop.

Paddle A device used to propel a boat. A paddle consists of a shaft with a blade on one or both ends.

Paddler A kayaker or canoeist.

Rapid A section of river where the river bed is steep. This increases the speed and power of the water flow.

Shaft The long part of a paddle that is gripped by the paddler.

Slalom A contest where paddlers negotiate a series of gates.

Slide Water flowing over an area of smooth bedrock.

Upstream Opposite to the direction a river is flowing.

Whirlpool A swirling body of water under a river's surface.

White water Turbulent water that is full of air. White water results from water flowing around and over obstacles in its path.

Index